Start Now:

Unlock the Money Value of Time

Jim D. Little

ISBN: 978-1-4834-1510-9 (sc)
ISBN: 978-1-4834-1511-6 (e)

Lulu Publishing Services rev. date: 9/26/2014

Contents

Introduction
Why You Should Start Saving and Employing Time Value Techniques Now   *1*

One
Living on a Cash Basis: What It Is and How You Get There   *6*

Two
Budgeting and Use of the Annual Resource Management Worksheet   *11*
    ~ Annual Resource Management Worksheet   *15*

Three
*Budgeting and Use of the Monthly Resource Management Worksheet
(MRMW)*   *16*
    ~ Monthly Resource Management Worksheet (MRMW)   *19*

Four
$1.00 Saved is $1.32 Earned   *21*

Five
Avoiding and Eliminating Consumer Debt   *24*

Six
Eliminating Home Mortgage Debt   *31*
    *~ New Home Buyer Amortization Schedule - Sample Home
      Mortgage (Regular 30 Year):
      Monthly Payments for First Year of Mortgage*   *36*
    *~ New Home Buyer Amortization Schedule - Sample Home
      Mortgage (30 Year): Biweekly Payments for First Year of
      Mortgage*   *40*
    *~ New Home Buyer Amortization Schedule - Sample Home
      Mortgage (30 Year): Biweekly Payments for Last Year of
      Mortgage*   *42*
    *~ New Home Buyer Amortization Schedule - Sample Home
      Mortgage (Regular 15 Year): Monthly Payments for First
      Year of Mortgage*   *46*
    *~ New Home Buyer Amortization Schedule - Sample Home
      Mortgage (Regular 15 Year): Monthly Payments for Last
      Year of Mortgage*   *47*

Seven

The Money Value of Time Part One: Investing a Single Sum of Money over Time   *49*

     ~ Future Value of $1   *54*

Eight

The Money Value of Time Part Two: Investing Sums of Money Regularly over Time   *56*

     ~ Future Value of an Ordinary Annuity of $1   *59*

Nine

The Money Value of Time Part Three: Multiplying the $Outcome through Higher Rates of Return   *61*

Ten

My Biggest Mistakes: Learn at My Expense   *65*

Eleven

Invest In Yourself   *69*

Twelve

Set Your Course and Write It Down   *73*

Why You Should Start Saving and Employing Time Value Techniques Now

Do you want to learn how to effectively control expenses, live on a cash basis, and eliminate debt? Do you desire to save money and build financial security but doubt that you can because your income is average? Are you young? If your answers to any of these questions are yes, then this book is a must read for you.

This book compels young adults to engage time now, while they have it, to build financial security for their futures. Time is a strong advantage in the financial equation for young adults. Yes, even the average earner who starts employing sound financial disciplines early can have a strong advantage in building future financial security.

The still-unfolding global financial crisis, recent years' turbulence in U.S. financial and real estate markets, and high unemployment rates have brought an awareness of how quickly the financial and economic landscape can change and instability can arise. You would think such events would have been a wake up call to change course regarding savings and spending habits. But have they changed? According to a survey released by Bankrate.com in June, 2013, things have not changed in the U.S. This survey of 1,000 adults indicates three quarters of Americans are living paycheck to paycheck, with little or no emergency savings. Expressed another way, only 24% of those surveyed had enough money in emergency savings to cover six months of expenses. Emergency savings is not the only measure of financial stability, but it is a fundamental indicator of preparedness should unexpected circumstances occur (loss of job, etc.).

The U.S. personal savings rate (computed as a percentage of personal disposable income), which has a direct correlation to the amount of emergency savings, has averaged approximately 4.0% for years 2008 through 2013. The average rate since 1959 is 6.87%.

Is a savings rate of 4.0% which is approximately 58% of the average of the last 53 years too low? I hope we don't have to find out the answer to that question through another set of trying experiences. I believe young adults have a great opportunity to strengthen America. Those I serve as clients in my CPA practice are aware of America's financial challenges, and I am confident they are up to the task of meeting them. Also, the feedback I am getting from these young clients confirms the desire for a financially-simple, debt-free, less-stress, steadily-improving financial life, which is exactly what this book attempts to help young adults achieve. I believe this book will be a valuable asset to its readers for the following reasons:

- Readers will learn how to (1) effectively control expenses, (2) live on a cash basis, and (3) eliminate debt. Accomplishing these objectives reduces fixed expenses and lowers the breakeven point (the point where income and expenses meet). This is important because when income exceeds breakeven, the excess is available for savings to fund financial goals that are more long-term in nature, such as buying a car or house, funding education for your children, or funding retirement for yourself. Having a low breakeven point, or a low level of fixed expenses, is a strong advantage in good times because a person can save more, and in bad times because he or she has a lower level of expenses and needs less to get by.
- The financial concept known as the "time value of money," in the context of interest earned, is restated and clarified in this book as "the money value of time." Knowledge of how this concept works for a person (when

saving) can make or save readers thousands over time. Readers will also learn that time will be your financial partner and will work for you if you start practicing sound financial disciplines early in life.

- The concepts and methodologies presented in the book have been designed to assist in overcoming many mental adversaries that can derail financial progress. Without question financial problems can create mental stress, anxiety, depression, hopelessness, etc. These issues can present very serious obstacles to financial progress. Indeed, the mental angle of the financial game should not be underestimated. One of the things that motivated me to write this book was an article I read approximately eight years ago about two college students. Both students committed suicide having been overwhelmed by the debts they had accumulated while in college; they could see no way to escape their burdens. I had two children in college at that time, a daughter and son, and I decided they would finish college without debt and, given the opportunity, I would use my knowledge to help other young adults escape such tragic fates. I am convinced a person can get the upper hand on these mental adversaries by employing principles that boost confidence in a person's ability to manage and therefore reduce stress and mental taxation. I believe these advantages are gained and strengthened by regular maintenance and management of a person's finances.

- Consistent application of the concepts and methodologies presented in the book should, over time, enable readers to gain knowledge of many of the key aspects of personal finance, confidence in their abilities to manage financially, and skills that will enable them to make steady progress toward financial security. Also, the

concepts and methodologies presented are not complex. They can be easily learned and primarily relate to spending and savings habits—spend less, save more, get out of debt, invest wisely, and *start now*.
- The book is written with the understanding that readers expect something they can implement, not just read for conceptual understanding. Therefore, implementation of critical concepts is explained step by step and, where necessary, supported with easy-to-understand worksheets or references to other helpful information.

The presentation of chapter material in this book follows a certain order of progression. It begins with the introduction of material to assist the young adult that has no expense budget, no long-term savings plan, no investments, little to no money, and is currently using credit cards or other debt to make ends meet. The book concludes with a chapter on goal setting and action steps with the purpose of encouraging readers to implement at least part, or perhaps all, of what they have learned from reading the book. Concepts are introduced in an order that build on one another, starting with the chapter on how to live on a cash basis. Should a person have already mastered the material in some of the early chapters, then they may find it more useful to skip ahead to a chapter more applicable to their current circumstances. However, regardless of where you begin your reading of the book, it is paramount to start working toward your financial future *now*.

In summary, my goals in writing the book are to do the following:

- Provide knowledge to the current generation of young adults which will enable them to lead more financially content and secure lives and contribute to the financial strength and stability of the nation in which they live.

- Equip young adults with the financial skills to manage their matters wisely and in turn assist others.
- That this book, or perhaps future modifications of it, will become commonly used personal finance curriculum in elementary and high schools and also colleges and universities.

CHAPTER 1

Living on a Cash Basis:
What It Is and How You Get There

The primary subjects addressed in this book are saving and spending concepts. I am going to begin with the latter, and I have a reason for this approach. I understand that as young adults, many of you reading this book may not yet be in a position to save and I don't want that to discourage you from starting the process of improving your financial life. In fact, you may be in the best position to gain the most from this book. My conclusion is this: *Get spending under control first and saving will be the natural result.*

Let's begin by defining "living on a cash basis." Living on a cash basis basically means paying your bills from the income you make; this is otherwise known as living within your means. It also means that you do not use debt that accumulates as a means to pay your bills. For example, if you were living on a cash basis you would not use a credit card to pay for your groceries and then not pay it off in full each month. On the other hand, if you used a credit card to pay for your groceries and then paid it off in full each month, then you would be considered to be living on a cash basis. In that case, you did not increase debt; rather, you just used the credit card for convenience and paid the credit card issuer rather than the grocery store directly.

The credit card example is used to clarify the definition of living on a cash basis. However, I will also take this opportunity to say something more regarding the use of credit cards. Use of credit cards is easy but often addictive, and it is a common pathway to over spending for many young adults. My advice is if you can't pay your credit card bill in full each month, then don't use one. Paying cash, by debit card, or by check may not be as convenient but it does limit the amount you spend to the amount you presently have. Some inconvenience may be necessary to provide the mechanism to get the desired result (e.g., "no pain, no gain").

Why would you want to live on a cash basis? If you are not living on a cash basis, then you are spending more than you make. If you continue to spend more than you make, then you are accumulating debt. Growing debt is creating a future problem for you or someone else. Probably the most daunting issue about growing debt is the ability to keep up with the rising monthly payments. The inability to make required monthly payments is normally the first signal that causes a person to realize they may be in trouble. Soon to follow are late notices, late fees, collection letters, collection calls, repossessions, default judgments, etc. Heard enough? I hope that you have. Another advantage to cash-basis living is that resourceful thinking is developed when options are limited. In my CPA practice, I have witnessed businessmen being much more careful and resourceful with their own capital than those who routinely borrowed. Another advantage of a low-to-no-debt business is greater financial ability to withstand difficult times.

OK, we have defined living on a cash basis and covered some good reasons for desiring to do so. But how do you get started? *Your first step to living on a cash basis is to make the decision to live that way.* Does that sound too simple or easy? Well, it is simple but may not be easy. Nonetheless, in order to begin the process of change you have to establish a starting point. That starting point is a decision; some refer to a decision of commitment as a quality decision. For most, that decision will be put to the test over and over again. You will most likely be tempted to yield to overspending and debt. Advertisements are full of enticements to push you beyond your means. For example, consider such incentives as:

- Low down payments.
- Easy credit terms.

- Easy monthly payments.
- No interest until X date.
- No monthly payment until X date.
- All credit accepted, etc.

I have noticed over the last decade as Americans have stretched further beyond their means or real ability to pay, that advertisements have become more creative and more seductive. Our current credit crisis in America has, however, brought to light the results of over use of credit—repossessions, foreclosures, short sales, judgments where asset values are less than amounts received by lenders when sold to satisfy debts, bankruptcies, etc. It can and has really gotten ugly and unpleasant.

So how do you avoid the risk of falling prey to such tactics? Again, make the decision to live within the cash income you have. I am not saying that a decision of commitment to do this will result in the ability to live on the cash basis by morning. It will likely take a while to adjust your spending habits to the point that you can live within your income or means. But a decision of commitment starts the process of change. Over time, as you see improvements, your resolve to live on a cash basis will strengthen. As you prioritize your expenses and eliminate those that are unnecessary, pay down and pay off debts, and start saving money you will know that you have made the right decision.

Let's look at the subject of the decision to live on a cash basis from another perspective: choose to limit your options. Let me offer an example from my childhood. I didn't really have a choice in this matter, but my options were limited. When I was a teenager, I wanted to buy my first car—a used (very used I found out) 1965 Pontiac GTO. Having no money I decided to discuss it with my father, thinking that perhaps he would help me. All I can remember him saying was, "You save up half, and I will take care of the other half." He gave me no other options.

He did not say he would help me get a loan or anything like that. I had to save up my half first and then he would help me. Well, it took a few months but I did save up my half, and he kept his word and took care of the difference. Unfortunately, the GTO was still available (I wonder why), and I bought it. I was out of it within six months (even a cool car gets old when it requires one expensive repair after another!) My next vehicle was a four-door 1965 Ford Custom 500; it looked just like a police cruiser. It wasn't a real babe magnet but it was dependable, and I was able to buy it with what I got for the GTO.

Through that experience my dad taught me two extremely valuable lessons. Lesson one: when paying cash is the only option that you have, you are forced to be more thoughtful and resourceful. In this case, I was a little short on thoughtfulness but I was resourceful. Because I determined to purchase the GTO, I was forced to use the only resource I had, which was my ability to work and earn wages. I want to underscore the significance of this point: *living on a cash basis causes you to think about and consider your purchases more carefully.* When you are using debt to acquire items it is much easier to say "yes" when sometimes the right decision is "no." Living on a cash basis does not guarantee that you will always make the right purchasing decisions. However, you are much more likely to make fewer bad decisions if debt is not an option because your decisions will probably be more thought out. Lesson two is that he changed my view about purchasing cars; I learned that you can pay cash for a car. I did not realize it at the time, but that change was to have continuing significance to me concerning the purchase of automobiles and avoidance of debt in general. During our thirty-nine year marriage, my wife and I have acquired fifteen vehicles, six used and nine new. Twelve of the vehicles were straight cash purchases, one was paid off within a year, and two were prepaid leases (my wife's ideas).

I am guessing that you are probably thinking that living on a cash basis sounds good but you are not yet convinced that you could commit to a decision to live that way. I believe that you can if you *start now*. I believe that because you are most likely young, eager to establish financial stability, and intelligent enough to know that spending more than you make leads to difficult paths ahead.

So how do you begin living on a cash basis? *Make the decision to do so*. It is really that simple. *Change your mind*. If you need more motivation, talk to people going through financial crises now. Don't be afraid to ask people questions. Consider asking the question, "If you had the opportunity to do it over again, would you live on a cash basis?" I believe that you will find most people will answer that question, "Absolutely!" So, in order to get started, make the decision of commitment that you will live on a cash basis. Having made that decision, you will need a plan of action to implement it, which leads us to our next chapter on budgeting or expense planning.

CHAPTER 2

Budgeting and Use of the Annual Resource Management Worksheet

Although it may be obvious to some, one might ask, what is a budget? Simply put, a budget is a spending plan. Creating a budget is a very important part of learning how to manage personal finances wisely. Budgeting is not just scorekeeping. Staying up to date (i.e., weekly) with your spending provides valuable data for decision making. If you have set spending limits and know where you are, it is much easier to resist the urge to impulse spend. The value of this concept cannot be over emphasized. Controlled spending frees up money, which can be saved or used to reduce debt. I suggest the following approach to budgeting in this order:

- Create an annual budget.
- Create monthly budgets each month.
- Monitor actual expenses each week and each month.

I have designed two worksheets to assist you in this process. The first is an "Annual Resource Management Worksheet" (ARMW), which is included at the end of this chapter, and the second is a "Monthly Resource Management Worksheet" (MRMW), which will be included in the following chapter. The Annual Resource Management Worksheet should be used to create your annual budget. Creating an annual budget gives you the "big picture" for the year and establishes where your money has been going. The basic information needed is your prior year's income tax returns, bank statements, check registers, credit card statements, and any other records of spending. Don't worry if you do not have all of these records; the most critical are the tax returns, but if you do not have them, copies of your W-2 or prior year earnings statements will suffice. The point is to get a general idea of how much you make and spend on an annual basis and to use this information as you create monthly budgets in the future.

Creating the annual budget for the first time will not be an exact science but will be useful in the education process and will produce a document well worth the time to create it. Use information from your tax returns, W-2s, or earnings statements to determine the total money you received the prior year. Reduce this amount by taxes withheld or paid to arrive at your net after tax income. Then include information regarding your cash balances at the beginning and end of the year to determine your estimated annual spending. For example, if you had an after tax income of $35,000 and beginning and end-of-year cash balances of $3,100 and $4,000 respectively, then your estimated annual spending could be computed as follows:

Cash balance, beginning of year	$3,100
Net after tax annual income	+ 35,000
Cash balance end of year	- 4,000
Estimated annual spending	= *$34,100*

If you have other sources of cash flow that do not show up on your tax returns like savings withdrawals, gifts from family, or loans, you should adjust for those amounts in computing your estimated annual spending. Completing the rest of the annual budget is relatively simple. You know what you spent in total for the prior year. Enter that amount as the total for the prior year's expenses column. Then fill in the line items for known amounts from your spending records and, finally, estimate remaining amounts spent to equal your total spending for the prior year.

Having completed your recap of prior year's expenses, now it is time to analyze. Be sure to exercise caution—you are now moving from an administrative to a management function. You are about to change your financial life. You should now analyze (look over, evaluate) your prior year's expenses and plan what you can change for the current year. If this is your first shot at expense control, you will most likely have several categories of opportunity. Remember, if you do not cut something, you do not free up any money to make progress (to save or reduce debt). Discretionary items normally provide the greatest opportunities for making immediate improvement. Examples of these are clothing, entertainment, eating out, groceries, cable or satellite television, utilities, commuting, or recreational activities. Some modifications of these to consider which may reduce your expenses are:

- Shop at thrift stores for clothing (I have a multi-millionaire client that does this).
- Eat in except for a couple of times per month (for most singles and couples this can prove to be significant).
- Make a list before grocery shopping and stick to it. Also, use coupons and buy items in bulk that you use often.
- Cut your cable bill by dropping some of those movie channels and opt to rent from the library for a while (good option for students) or use Redbox.
- Turn up the thermostat a degree or two higher in the summer and a degree or two lower in the winter to help with utility costs (Try 68 degrees in winter and 78 degrees in summer; this really works for our house).
- Shop around for better prices on auto and homeowner's insurance.
- Perform regular maintenance on your vehicles (oil changes, etc.). This generally reduces overall vehicle costs and helps vehicles last longer.
- Carpool as much as possible or use public transportation to save on fuel costs. Plan your trips around town before going out in order to accomplish more per trip.

- Prepare your lunches and snacks at home for taking to work or school. Consider cutting the expensive lattes and make coffee at home as well. Savings on these small purchases can add up over time.
- When deciding on weekend entertainment, opt for inviting friends over for a game or movie night instead of going out for expensive dinners and movies.
- Try planning your recreational activities around outings that cost little or no money, such as museums, parks, free concerts, art shows, etc. (Check your local newspaper for free event listings.)
- Plan vacations ahead of time and look for the best deals online.

When you have finished your analysis, enter your planned changes for the current year in the column on the ARMW entitled "Current Year Adjustments." Add or subtract these amounts to or from your prior year's expenses and enter the resulting amounts in the column "Current Year Annual Budget." Congratulations! You have now completed your annual budget and are ready to move to monthly budgeting and resource management.

Annual Resource Management Worksheet

Expense Categories	Prior Year's Expenses	Current Year Adjustments	Current Year Annual Budget
Giving/Charity	_____	_____	_____
Mortgage/Rent	_____	_____	_____
Homeowner's/Renter's Insurance	_____	_____	_____
Utilities	_____	_____	_____
Home Repairs/ Improvements	_____	_____	_____
Property Taxes	_____	_____	_____
Automobile – Note Payments	_____	_____	_____
Auto Insurance	_____	_____	_____
Auto – Gas & Repairs	_____	_____	_____
Phone	_____	_____	_____
Groceries	_____	_____	_____
Life Insurance	_____	_____	_____
Medical Insurance/ Prescriptions	_____	_____	_____
Doctor's Prescriptions	_____	_____	_____
Other Medical Expense	_____	_____	_____
Dental Expenses	_____	_____	_____
Dental Insurance	_____	_____	_____
Installment Notes	_____	_____	_____
Credit Card Debts	_____	_____	_____
Other Debts	_____	_____	_____
Savings	_____	_____	_____
Clothing	_____	_____	_____
*Weekly Running Totals	[_____]	[_____]	[_____]

* This category would include items that you may not care to track individually but do recur frequently, such as lunches out, laundry and dry cleaning, and other small out-of-pocket expenses. You may want to add additional categories of expense to suit your personal needs or desires. The objective is to document meaningful information relative to your personal expenses.

CHAPTER 3

Budgeting and Use of the Monthly Resource Management Worksheet (MRMW)

Having created your current annual budget, you are now prepared to begin monthly budgeting and using the monthly resource management worksheet (MRMW). The worksheet is provided at the end of this chapter. I take this opportunity to emphasize monthly expense management through use of the MRMW. This process enhances your skills as an expense manager and, through weekly documentation of actual expenses and comparison to budget amounts, helps keep you informed as to where you are each month and each week.

Create your monthly budget using the MRMW just prior to or at the beginning of each month. By referring to the current-year budget you have prepared and the knowledge of expenses that will be coming up during the current month, compute and enter the amounts in the column "Monthly Budget." It is OK if some expenses come up later in the month that you did not enter as part of your monthly budget to begin with. Just update your monthly budget amounts when these changes occur. What I am referring to primarily are expenses you didn't think about when you created your monthly budget, such as an unexpected insurance bill or emergencies such as appliance or auto repairs for which you might not have budgeted enough. I am not referring to discretionary expenses such as entertainment, road trips, clothing, etc., which should normally be kept within budget amounts or the process fails to produce the desired results (e.g., expenses kept within reasonable limits).

The next step in managing your financial resources is to pay all bills that are due at the end of each week if at all possible. This is very important, and I want to bring to your attention the significance and hidden value of this practice now. The point is that personal financial management is not only a numbers game but a mental game. As long as you have unpaid bills piling up, they tend to worry you and weaken your frame of mind financially. Once paid, however, bills are put behind you, no longer to linger in the background of your mind and to create anxiety. Instead, with bills paid, your frame of mind significantly improves and you gain confidence in your ability to win this game. In other words, paying your bills promptly lightens the mental load. Once you have paid your bills at the end of the week, post your actual expenses to the appropriate weekly column on the MRMW.

The final number crunching step is to complete the "cash analysis" section at the bottom of the MRMW. This procedure forces you to check your math and make sure you have accounted for all your expenses for the week (total expenses amount). Normally the process of completing the MRMW takes no longer than an hour per week if you run all of your payments/ expenses through a single checking account. If you use more than one account, you would need to combine amounts and post summarized totals to the MRMW. I suggest use of a single account for paying your household bills, if possible, in order to reduce the time required for the overall process. However, don't give up if this is not feasible; just commit to spending a little more time in the recapping of your numbers.

After you have completed posting of the current week's expenses, compare these actual weekly amounts to the budget amounts for the month to assess how you are doing. How much budget you have left in discretionary items should guide your spending decisions over the remainder of the month. *These decisions are extremely important considered in the aggregate over time, as this ongoing process of prioritizing expenses and evaluating their necessity sharpens your financial management skills.*

Another byproduct of this weekly process is that in looking over your planned (budget) and actual expenses each week you are becoming more educated and knowledgeable as to the specific expenditures that are using up your resources. Thoughts begin to arise such as, "I wonder what life would be like without this car payment or credit card payment?" "Are there more effective insurance (home, auto, life, etc.) options we should consider?" Whatever it is, if it's unproductive and using up your resources that could be going for more important things such as college or retirement savings, a paid-for vacation, etc., you will most likely begin to think of ways to eliminate unnecessary expenditures and reduce those that are necessary. Such thinking will lead to action and will start the process of change. This process builds upon itself. Don't make the mistake of thinking a small step is insignificant. Remember the old adage, "Inch by inch it's a cinch, but by the yard it's hard."

On the final week of the month, summarize your actual expenses (total column at the far right) on the MRMW. Compare your total actual to total budget expenses. How did you do? Did you learn anything that will help you reduce expenses in the month or year(s) ahead? At this point I suggest that you start a follow-up list. Sometimes you can have some great ideas but because they were not written down, they are forgotten and never acted upon. Write down matters that you wish to investigate and keep them on top in a file where you keep these MRMWs for the year. Then next week when you open your file to work on your MRMW, your follow-up list will be the first thing you see.

Monthly Resource Management Worksheet (MRMW)

Expense Categories	Monthly Budget	Week 1	Week 2	Week 3	Week 4	Week 5	Monthly Totals
Giving/Charity							
Mortgage/Rent							
Homeowner's/Renter's Insurance							
Utilities							
Home Repairs/Improvements							
Property Taxes							
Automobile – Note Payments							
Auto Insurance							
Auto – Gas & Repairs							
Phone							
Groceries							
Life Insurance							
Medical Insurance/Prescriptions							
Doctor's Prescriptions							
Other Medical Expense							
Dental Expenses							
Dental Insurance							

Installment Notes

Credit Card Debts

Other Debts

Savings

Clothing

*Weekly Running

Total Expenses

Cash Analysis

Cash, beginning of week

(Plus) Deposits

(Minus) Total Expenses Above

(Equals) Cash, End of Week

*This category would include items that you may not care to track individually but do recur frequently such as lunches out, laundry and dry cleaning and other small out of pocket expenses. You may want to add additional categories of expense to suit your personal needs or desires. The objective is meaningful information relative to your personal expenses.

CHAPTER 4

$1.00 Saved is $1.32 Earned

I'm sure you have heard of the familiar phrase "A penny saved is a penny earned," often attributed to Benjamin Franklin. Franklin may not have actually been the one to coin this phrase but he was known to have used it and was also known as a wise and wealthy man and also author of one of the first American books on personal finance, *The Way to Wealth*. Although it may be obvious, I consider the basic gist of this phrase to be that it is wise to save.

Now, I am not attempting to put my writing on a level with that of Benjamin Franklin, but I do want to pick up on the subject of savings and to address it from a CPA's tax perspective. I also want to clarify that I am addressing the subject as it relates to personal finances; that is, the arena of life where taxes generally have to be paid before money is available for spending.

In Franklin's day there were no income taxes; therefore, a penny saved was truly a penny earned. Most of us who work in the United States and earn wages now pay social security, Medicare, federal income and state income taxes. Therefore, to earn a penny we must pay those taxes out of our wages earned to arrive at our wages net of taxes, otherwise known as "net pay." To bring the "penny saved is a penny earned" phrase up to current day reality including taxes, it would be something like, "A penny saved is a penny of net pay earned." You may ask, just how much difference do the taxes make? The standard answer from a CPA is "It depends," which is really quite true. It depends on your level of income, filing status, deductions, etc. But to keep it simple and relevant to young adults, let's take the example of an individual who in 2012 earned wages of $45,000, was single, took the standard deduction, claimed an exemption for himself/herself, and lived in Georgia. The tax rates for this individual would be:

Social Security and Medicare Tax	7.65%
Federal Income Tax	11.00%
Ga. Income Tax	5.00%
Total	23.65%

Using these tax rates an individual would need to earn $1.32 to net one dollar after tax, as follows:

Gross Pay	$1.32
Social Security and Medicare Tax	- $.10
Federal Income Tax	- $.15
Ga. Income Tax	- $.07
Net Pay	$1.00

Now, let's re-phrase the quote: "A dollar saved is one dollar and thirty-two cents earned." Or, "A dollar saved is worth 32 more cents than a dollar earned." So what is the point? The point is this: when it comes to personal finances, a dollar saved and a dollar earned are not equivalent because of taxes. So Franklin's wisdom regarding saving would be more relevant today because $1.00 saved is worth more than $1.00 earned.

How can this information be applied to help you? Reducing personal expenses is more valuable, dollar for dollar, than earning more income. Therefore, it is important to know what you are spending and eliminate expenses that are unnecessary. In chapter two, the importance of and how to develop an annual budget was explained. The annual budget is a great place to start looking for expenses to eliminate. Think about it, to earn more money you have to work more. Working is generally hard and very time consuming. Reducing unnecessary expenses is generally easier. If you have never prepared an annual budget and gone through the process of eliminating the unnecessary stuff, you probably have a field ripe for harvest.

This is not a game only for penny pinchers. Good business managers continuously employ techniques to reduce the unnecessary. Also, some people are just better managers than earners. If this is your bent, saving money is where you can shine. So what are you waiting for? There may be easy pickings in the household budget. So get started now to find them and give yourself a raise "net of taxes."

CHAPTER 5

Avoiding and Eliminating Consumer Debt

The subject of avoiding debt is also discussed in the previous chapter "Living on a Cash Basis"; therefore, re-reading or scanning it over before reading this chapter may provide a good introduction to avoiding and eliminating consumer debt. Personal Debt is generally classified under two primary categories:

- Home mortgages—eliminating home mortgage debt will be covered in the next chapter.
- Consumer debt which includes all other personal debt. Consumer debt includes such items as school loans, vehicle loans, loans for furniture and other household items, general unsecured loans, and credit cards.

Business debt is also a type of debt an individual can owe but is beyond the scope of this book. However, some of the debt elimination techniques explained for consumer and mortgage debt may be useful for those with business debt.

Here is my summary of personal debt education: It's easy to get into but hard to get out of; personal debt should be avoided if at all possible. One exception is home mortgage debt if certain criteria are met, which I will explain later in the chapter. So, in summary, I advise you to make every effort to avoid consumer debt unless it is absolutely necessary. But why exactly should one avoid consumer debt? I offer two primary reasons:

- It most likely causes your net worth to go down, which means you are backing up financially. If you are spending more than you make, then you are creating debt and reducing your net worth. Your net worth is equal to the value of your assets less the amount of your liabilities or debt. In addition to amounts borrowed, interest is charged on debt unless it's a special deal (normally a family member or friend). Interest on credit card debt is normally one of the highest interest debts an individual carries. Therefore, if you are accumulating debt (not paying it off each month) your net worth is being reduced by amounts borrowed plus interest that is charged on the outstanding debt balance—that is, unless your assets are increasing in value at a greater amount than your debt. This is unlikely for most young adults whose assets are generally bank accounts, vehicles, and household items that typically do not increase in value.

- It creates an obligation against future income you may not have. Decisions about debt involve presuming the ability to make all of the payments. If your budget is already tight, and/or your income is uncertain, these "up-front" indicators are telling you that you most likely won't have such ability, or the experience will prove financially difficult.

Debt can operate like a trap. "Wow," you may say, "you really are against consumer debt, aren't you?" Yes, that's right. I am. It looks like an easy way to get what you need or want but once you enter the trap and take the bait, the door closes and you are ensnared by the payments. I believe most young adults have other options which will result in better long-term outcomes for them.

Earlier in the chapter, I stated my one exception to debt avoidance was home mortgage debt if certain criteria were met. Also, I am speaking of first mortgage debt only, not second mortgages, home equity lines of credit, etc. The reason I make it my one exception is that a person normally has to pay for housing whether they buy or rent. In other words, you have to have shelter and you normally have to pay for it. Other items for which you may be tempted to borrow generally have more options (buy used, don't buy at all, wait, etc.) and are not as necessary or not necessary at all.

I realize there are a number of factors to consider when selecting housing, such as market value, distance to work, school district, neighborhood safety, etc. However, if you have evaluated those factors and others considered important to you and have made a preliminary decision to buy, I recommend that your selection meet criteria that I term "lowest estimated net costs." I suggest that you perform a simple analysis of costs of purchasing vs. renting over 10 years, which is close to the average numbers of years (9) that people lived in their purchased homes as determined in 2011.

The following example demonstrates the methodology I recommend in analyzing the costs and assumes you purchase a home for $150,000, pay 10% down, and finance the remainder over 30 years at 4.5% interest. The example also assumes real estate taxes, insurance, and repairs totaling $5,500 per year. The example calculation is as follows:

Estimated Net Costs to Purchase:

Down Payment	$15,000
Mortgage payments @ $684 per month (principal and interest)	$82,080
Taxes, insurance, and repairs	$55,000
Total estimated out-of-pocket costs	$152,080
Value in ten years (no change)	$150,000
Mortgage balance after ten years	-$108,120
Net value of home	$41,880
Net costs to purchase (out-of-pocket costs less net value of home)	*$110,200*

Estimated Cost to Rent:

Rent payments @ $1,250 per month	$150,000
Estimated savings to purchase	*$39,800*

Under the above example analysis, purchasing saves approximately $40,000 over renting; therefore, it results in the "lowest estimated net costs." For the calculation I used data for housing in my area, an east Atlanta suburb, and obtained most of it from a realtor. I computed the mortgage payments and balance using amortization software (you can access this type of software online for free). The value in 10 years (no change) was a guess, but you should do your best to obtain an accurate estimate.

I would like to shift the focus of the remainder of this chapter to eliminating consumer debt. The initial approach I recommend to reducing consumer debt is what I term the strategic payment plan. It involves listing your debts, negotiating with creditors where possible and developing and implementing a strategic payment plan. It assumes you intend to pay your creditors in full or a negotiated amount, and that you do not intend to file for bankruptcy protection. If you are considering bankruptcy protection I recommend that you consult with a qualified bankruptcy attorney before implementing a payment plan for creditors.

To begin the process of developing a strategic payment plan, I recommend that you first list your debts, noting the total amounts due, monthly payment amounts, number of remaining payments, and interest rates. To begin with, rank your debts in order of the total amount due, smallest to largest. Next, begin the process of contacting and negotiating with each creditor. *Start with the smallest one first.* This process will most likely not be easy but hopefully fruitful and educational. Your objectives are reduced amounts due and/or reduced interest rates. Some ideas for creditor negotiation are as follows:

- Start your conversation with a statement such as, "I am serious about paying my obligation to you, but my resources are limited at this time. Are there any options available for reducing my obligation or interest rate?"
- For creditors with smaller amounts due, you may also suggest "I have paid on this account for quite some time and paid considerable interest, could you just write off the balance?"
- For debts with higher interest rates, which you have the ability to pay more on, suggest, "If I can find a way to increase my monthly payment, will you consider reducing my balance due or interest rate, or eliminating interest if I pay you off in X months?"

I'll give you a recent example from my CPA practice. One of my clients had a credit card liability of approximately $33,000. The interest rate was 25.2%, and the minimum monthly payment required was $1,647. The interest on this account was running approximately $672 per month, and when payments were late, a late fee of $39 was also charged. Furthermore, the client's business was in a slump and the minimum payments could not be made. So what happened? The client contacted the credit card issuer and reached the following agreement:

- The account was closed for future purchases and advances.
- The interest rate was reduced to zero.
- The monthly minimum payments were reset to $549 for a term of sixty months which was the term required to payoff the account.

Was the lender contact worth the effort? I will let you be the judge. According to my calculations the interest saved over the five-year payout term will total approximately $24,500. My comment to my client was "Well done."

As you start working on your list and negotiating with your creditors, you will gain knowledge and education on what creditors want and what options you have. Modify your remaining negotiations to include this additional knowledge gained. After you have completed your creditor negotiations, structure your list of debts to strategically reduce them in the most rapid order possible. Usually this means reducing smallest to largest debt balances in that order. Should you have extra to pay on your debts, apply that to the smallest balances first unless you have committed the extra to more effectively reducing your debt via your creditor negotiations. *As you pay off a debt, add the amount you were previously paying for that debt to your next largest debt until it is paid off. Then, repeat the process over and over until your creditors are paid in full.* This process is often referred to as "snowballing" payments. You continue to pay the same overall total on your debts from start to finish. In short, here is a summary of the strategic payment method for eliminating debt:

- List your debts.
- Negotiate with your creditors.

- Structure your strategic debt payments.
- Implement your plan (e.g., "snowball" your debt payments).

After having negotiated with creditors and implemented a strategic payment plan, if you are still left with high interest debts (perhaps credit cards) or unfavorable payment terms, I suggest one other approach to consumer debt elimination, and this is *debt consolidation*. It may not be an available option but, if it is, I recommend it as a last option. The reason is that debt consolidation may ease the creditor stress and reduce the interest paid, but it may not cure the underlying debt illness. What I am trying to say is that debt consolidation can be quick and easy, but if you don't implement a process of maximum payments to eliminate the debt as soon as possible, you may be tempted to be happy with the consolidated debt payment but have developed no resolve to eliminate your debts ASAP and/or perhaps incur additional debt. However, if your resolve is strong to reduce debt ASAP, a consolidation loan for debts with high interest rates and/or unfavorable payment terms may be an effective solution to eliminate that segment of your debt.

CHAPTER 6

Eliminating Home Mortgage Debt

Home mortgage debt is usually the last debt a person addresses in a debt elimination plan. It is generally last because excess money is normally first used to reduce consumer debts, for reasons such as higher interest rates and eliminating the monthly payments faster because of the lower amount of debt. I will present three different techniques for eliminating home mortgage debt in this chapter.

The first home mortgage elimination technique that I would like to explain involves *making one mortgage payment each month and paying extra principal with each payment*. Before getting into the details, however, I would like to share my personal experience with you because this is the technique my wife and I used to eliminate our 30-year mortgage in less than ten years. The following is my story with a little extra background data as well.

When I was a student at Auburn University over 30 years ago studying for my degree in Accounting, I took a "Time Value of Money" course. I was fascinated with what I learned then, and yet I must have forgotten everything the moment I walked out of the last class. The wake-up call came for me in 1989. My wife and I had been married for 15 years and just sold our first home after having paid on the related 30-year mortgage for 13 years. Over the 13-year period we had paid a total of $44,000 in principal and interest payments; $6,000 of that was principal (debt reduction) and $38,000 was interest. Wow! That was astonishing to me—that over the course of 13 years we had only paid off $6,000 of our mortgage debt. I determined something was going to change on the 30-year mortgage we now had on our second home.

It was at the same time, the spring of 1989, that our pastor asked me to teach a class over the summer on the subject of how to get out of debt. I wasn't feeling very qualified at the time but accepted the challenge anyway. My focus then was on home mortgage amortization; I do not remember anything I taught on eliminating consumer debt. As I prepared to teach the class, I remembered the story of "David and Goliath" in the *Bible*. I began to view all those mortgage payments as Goliath and myself as David. A 30-year mortgage including 360 monthly payments can be very intimidating, but armed with the knowledge of how mortgage amortization works (formerly dormant but recently acutely awakened, due to the experience of my first home mortgage) I was ready to engage the "enemy." My battle strategy was to pay off the 30-year mortgage in 15 years. The rocks I used to slay the giant (the mortgage) were extra principal payments each month. I was also emboldened through David's example to speak to the giant (the mortgage) something to the effect of, "You are coming down!" Well, as crazy as it might sound, that strategy worked. We paid off the mortgage in less than 10 years.

I do not remember any testimonies from others in the class I taught the summer of 1989. However, I taught an updated class on debt elimination to a church group sometime around 1995 or 1996. About 5 years later, one of the ladies in attendance (probably not over 40 years old) approached my wife in a grocery store and told her that she and her husband had just paid off their mortgage. In only five years they had put this method to work and paid off their mortgage which was, as I recall, somewhere between $50,000 and $75,000. *Wow, that's fast!* A big reason why this method is so effective, I believe, is that a person develops determination and confidence because progress can be seen as each extra payment is made. I am certain our friends from the church group became more confident in their abilities to succeed financially through this accomplishment.

Now I want to give you the details so you can use this method to eliminate *your* home mortgage. First of all, you need a copy of your mortgage amortization schedule. This is the schedule that lists all payments required under the mortgage, the date each payment is due, the principal and interest portions of each payment, and the remaining balance of the mortgage after each payment. If not included with your mortgage documents, you should be able to get a copy from your lender. You should also communicate with your lender to make sure there is no pre-payment penalty associated with your mortgage (most lenders allow pre-payments without penalty) and the details of how to identify your principal pre-payments when submitting.

Next, study the amortization schedule to see how the mortgage reduction is calculated. I have included copies of monthly payment schedules for years one and thirty from a $135,000, 30-year, 4.5% mortgage so you can get an understanding now while reading this book of the concept of declining amortization and interest savings when prepaying. Please take a brief look at these amortization schedule pages that follow this example explanation. Now, you must first decide how much extra principal you plan to pay each month or how fast you want to pay down your mortgage. Let's assume you can afford to pay an extra $200 or so per month to start with, and you want to eliminate your mortgage in 15 years rather than thirty. In order to do that you need to make two principal payments per month (30 divided by 15 = 2). So your first monthly payment amount would be $862.48 which is the total payment amount of $684.03 for payment number one plus the next month's (Pmt. No. 2) principal of $178.45. Your second monthly payment would be $863.82, which is the total payment amount of $684.03 for payment number three, plus the next month's (Pmt. No. 4) principal of $179.79. Notice what has happened after making these two payments: the mortgage balance has been reduced by the four principal payments to $134,284.86, and the interest amounts for Pmt. No. 2 and Pmt. No. 4 totaling $1,009.82 have been skipped, i.e., eliminated or saved.

If you continue this process of making one extra principal payment each month on a 30-year mortgage, it will be paid off in 15 years if you start with the first payment. The total for each monthly payment submitted using this technique will gradually grow over the fifteen-year period which reflects the increasing amount of principal that is paid with each payment on the lower total principal balance. The monthly payments including the extra month's principal for the $135,000 mortgage example presented would be as follows:

End of year three	$915.93
End of year six	$987.65
End of year nine	$1,081.57
End of year twelve	$1,204.53
End of year fifteen	$1,358.36

As indicated, the monthly amounts increase gradually over the time periods and hopefully your income would as well, providing for the necessary additional payment amounts. But let's say you only can make the payments required using this technique through year nine. At that point, twelve years of payments remain; therefore, you have reduced your 30-year mortgage to 21 years in all (the nine for which extra payments were made and the twelve remaining). Also, interest saved over the nine-year period would total $44,320. Not bad!

However, should you make extra principal payments using this technique starting with the first required payment under the mortgage and continue doing so for 15 years, the mortgage will be paid in full after only 15 years and interest saved will total $55,497. A summary of amounts paid and saved follows:

	Total Payments	Total Interest Expense	Principal Reduction
*Regular 30-year mortgage	$246,247	$111,247	$135,000
Technique of paying next month's principal with regular payment amount	$190,750	$55,750	$135,000
Savings	$55,497	$55,497	$0

*From the second page of the amortization schedule presented that follows this example explanation, "Sample Home Mortgage (Regular 30 year)."

New Home Buyer Amortization Schedule - Sample Home Mortgage (Regular 30 Year): Monthly Payments for First Year of Mortgage

Principal:	135,000.00					Annual Interest Rate:	4.500
Term:	360 Payments					Payments Per Year:	12

Pmt. No.	Due Date:	Date Paid	Payment Amount	Interest Expense	Principal Reduction	Payoff Amount
						135,000.00
1	01/28/13		684.03	506.25	177.78	134,822.22
2	02/28/13		684.03	505.58	178.45	134,643.77
3	03/28/13		684.03	504.91	179.12	134,464.65
4	04/28/13		684.03	504.24	179.79	134,284.86
5	05/28/13		684.03	503.57	180.46	134,104.40
6	06/28/13		684.03	502.89	181.14	133,923.26
7	07/28/13		684.03	502.21	181.82	133,741.44
8	08/28/13		684.03	501.53	182.50	133,558.94
9	09/28/13		684.03	500.85	183.18	133,375.76
10	10/28/13		684.03	500.16	183.87	133,191.89
11	11/28/13		684.03	499.47	184.56	133,007.33
12	12/28/13		684.03	498.78	185.25	132,822.08
Sub-total			8,208.36	6,030.44	2,177.92	132,822.08

New Home Buyer Amortization Schedule - Sample Home Mortgage (Regular 30 Year): Monthly Payments for Last Year of Mortgage

349	01/28/42	684.03	30.03	654.00	7,354.30
350	02/28/42	684.03	27.58	656.45	6,697.85
351	03/28/42	684.03	25.12	658.91	6,038.94
352	04/28/42	684.03	22.65	661.38	5,377.56
353	05/28/42	684.03	20.17	663.86	4,713.70
354	06/28/42	684.03	17.68	666.35	4,047.35
355	07/28/42	684.03	15.18	668.85	3,378.50
356	08/28/42	684.03	12.67	671.36	2,707.14
357	09/28/42	684.03	10.15	673.88	2,033.26
358	10/28/42	684.03	7.62	676.41	1,356.85
359	11/28/42	684.03	5.09	678.94	677.91
360	12/28/42	684.03	2.54	677.91	0.00
Sub-total		8,208.36	196.48	8,008.30	0.00
Total		246,247.22	111,247.22	135,000.00	0.00

The technique of paying next month's principal with your regular payment amount can be utilized over different time periods for payoff. For example, to pay off a 30-year mortgage in 10 years, then the regular monthly payment plus two extra monthly principal payments need to be made (30 divided by 10 = 3). From my experience, once a person starts using this technique and begins to see results, they are motivated to continue. I like this method of mortgage elimination for several reasons:

1) It's flexible. Pay extra principal if you can; if you can't, you are not locked into higher payments.
2) It generally requires no change in your mortgage agreements. Clear with your lender before starting, however.
3) With an amortization schedule it's easy to determine how much extra principal to pay and track progress on mortgage reduction. The amortization schedule is also useful for checking amounts per lender's annual statement of interest and principal.

The second mortgage reduction technique I would like to present requires splitting your regular mortgage payment in half and paying the one half amounts biweekly (not bimonthly). This process results in making 26 half payments per year or the equivalent of 13 regular monthly payments. Please refer to the pages which present payments for the first and last year for the sample amortization schedule found following this example explanation; the sample mortgage data presented is based on the same mortgage as presented for the regular 30-year mortgage explained in the previous example. In our present example, the biweekly payments were determined by dividing the regular 30-year mortgage payment of $684.03 by 2. Consistent employment of this elimination technique from the start of the mortgage reduces a $135,000, 30-year term, 4.5% interest rate mortgage to a term of 25 years, 6 months and saves $18,925 in interest. A summary of amounts paid and saved are as follows:

	Total Payments	Interest Expense	Principal Reduction
*Regular 30-year mortgage	$246,247	$111,247	$135,000
**Technique of paying bi-weekly (26 half-regular payments per year)	$227,322	$92,322	$135,000
Savings	$18,925	$18,925	$0

*From amortization schedule presented previously, "Sample Home Mortgage (Regular 30 Year)."

**From the second page of the amortization schedule following this example explanation, "Sample Home Mortgage (30 Year – Biweekly Payments)."

New Home Buyer Amortization Schedule - Sample Home Mortgage
(30 Year): Biweekly Payments for First Year of Mortgage

Principal:	135,000.00			Annual Interest Rate:		4.500
Term:	665 Payments			Payments Per Year:		26

Pmt. No.	Due Date:	Date Paid	Payment Amount	Interest Expense	Principal Reduction	Payoff Amount
						135,000.00
1	01/14/13	_____	342.02	233.65	108.37	134,891.63
2	01/28/13	_____	342.02	233.47	108.55	134,783.08
3	02/11/13	_____	342.02	233.28	108.74	134,674.34
4	02/25/13	_____	342.02	233.09	108.93	134,565.41
5	03/11/13	_____	342.02	232.90	109.12	134,456.29
6	03/25/13	_____	342.02	232.71	109.31	134,346.98
7	04/08/13	_____	342.02	232.52	109.50	134,237.48
8	04/22/13	_____	342.02	232.33	109.69	134,127.79
9	05/06/13	_____	342.02	232.14	109.88	134,017.91
10	05/20/13	_____	342.02	231.95	110.07	133,907.84
11	06/03/13	_____	342.02	231.76	110.26	133,797.58
12	06/17/13	_____	342.02	231.57	110.45	133,687.13

#	Date				
13	07/01/13	342.02	231.38	110.64	133,576.49
14	07/15/13	342.02	231.19	110.83	133,465.66
15	07/29/13	342.02	231.00	111.02	133,354.64
16	08/12/13	342.02	230.81	111.21	133,243.43
17	08/26/13	342.02	230.61	111.41	133,132.02
18	09/09/13	342.02	230.42	111.60	133,020.42
19	09/23/13	342.02	230.23	111.79	132,908.63
20	10/07/13	342.02	230.03	111.99	132,796.64
21	10/21/13	342.02	229.84	112.18	132,684.46
22	11/04/13	342.02	229.65	112.37	132,572.09
23	11/18/13	342.02	229.45	112.57	132,459.52
24	12/02/13	342.02	229.26	112.76	132,346.76
25	12/16/13	342.02	229.06	112.96	132,233.80
26	12/30/13	342.02	228.87	113.15	132,120.65
Sub-total		8,892.52	6,030.44	2,177.92	132,822.08

New Home Buyer Amortization Schedule - Sample Home Mortgage
(30 Year): Biweekly Payments for Last Year of Mortgage

Principal:	135,000.00			Annual Interest Rate:		4.500
Term:	665 Payments			Payments Per Year:		26
Pmt. No.	Due Date:	Date Paid	Payment Amount	Interest Expense	Principal Reduction	Payoff Amount
640	07/13/37	_____	342.02	14.84	327.18	8,244.89
641	07/27/37	_____	342.02	14.27	327.75	7,917.14
642	08/10/37	_____	342.02	13.70	328.32	7,588.82
643	08/24/37	_____	342.02	13.13	328.89	7,259.93
644	09/07/37	_____	342.02	12.57	329.45	6,930.48
645	09/21/37	_____	342.02	12.00	330.02	6,600.46
646	10/05/37	_____	342.02	11.42	330.60	6,269.86
647	10/19/37	_____	342.02	10.85	331.17	5,938.69
648	11/02/37	_____	342.02	10.28	331.74	5,606.95
649	11/16/37	_____	342.02	9.70	332.32	5,274.63
650	11/30/37	_____	342.02	9.13	332.89	4,941.74

651	12/14/37	——	342.02	8.55	333.47	4,608.27
652	12/28/37	——	342.02	7.98	334.04	4,274.23
653	01/11/38	——	342.02	7.40	334.62	3,939.61
654	01/25/38	——	342.02	6.82	335.20	3,604.41
655	02/08/38	——	342.02	6.24	335.78	3,268.63
656	02/22/38	——	342.02	5.66	336.36	2,932.27
657	03/08/38	——	342.02	5.08	336.94	2,595.33
658	03/22/38	——	342.02	4.49	337.53	2,257.80
659	04/05/38	——	342.02	3.91	338.11	1,919.69
660	04/19/38	——	342.02	3.32	338.70	1,580.99
661	05/03/38	——	342.02	2.74	339.28	1,241.71
662	05/17/38	——	342.02	2.15	339.87	901.84
663	05/31/38	——	342.02	1.56	340.46	561.38
664	06/14/38	——	342.02	0.97	341.05	220.33
665	06/28/38	——	220.71	0.38	220.33	0.00
Sub-total			8,771.21	199.14	8572.07	0.00
Total			227,321.99	92,321.99	135,000.00	0.00

Facts regarding the bi-weekly payment technique of amortization to consider:

- It does not require a significant amount of extra money to implement (equivalent to one regular monthly payment per year).
- The term reduction and savings are more modest than the first technique presented, but nevertheless significant enough to justify the hassle of making the split payments.
- This technique will likely require loan modification; therefore, do not implement before making the necessary arrangements with your lender. When making such arrangements, however, inquire whether flexibility to increase the biweekly amounts could be incorporated into this loan modification. This flexibility would allow you to accelerate the mortgage reduction by increasing payments should your income allow it in later years without having to modify loan documents again.
- Some lenders charge fees (one time or annual) for handling this type of loan amortization; therefore, these need to be evaluated relative to interest savings to determine if the net result is worth it.

The third and final mortgage reduction technique I would like to present is the most simple of all. Decide in advance your desired term of payout (20 year, 15 year, etc.), and have your mortgage set up that way. Keep in mind, though, that you are committed to the required payments. Using our previous $135,000, 4.5% interest rate mortgage example, choosing a 15-year term results in required monthly payments of $1,032.74 per month rather than $684.03 as under the regular 30-year mortgage. A summary of amounts paid and saved over the regular 30-year mortgage is as follows:

	Total Payments	Interest Expense	Principal Reduction
*Regular 30-year mortgage	$246,247	$111,247	$135,000
**15-year mortgage	$185,893	$50,893	$135,000
Savings	$60,354	$60,354	$0

*From amortization schedule presented previously, "Sample Home Mortgage (Regular 30 Year)."

**From amortization schedule presented following this example explanation, "Sample Home Mortgage (Regular 15 year)."

New Home Buyer Amortization Schedule - Sample Home Mortgage
(Regular 15 Year): Monthly Payments for First Year of Mortgage

Principal:	135,000.00		Annual Interest Rate:		4.500
Term:	180 Payments		Payments Per Year:		12

Pmt. No.	Due Date:	Date Paid	Payment Amount	Interest Expense	Principal Reduction	Payoff Amount
						135,000.00
1	01/14/13	_____	1,032.74	506.25	526.49	134,473.51
2	02/14/13	_____	1,032.74	504.28	528.46	133,945.05
3	03/14/13	_____	1,032.74	502.29	530.45	133,414.60
4	04/14/13	_____	1,032.74	500.30	532.44	132,882.16
5	05/14/13	_____	1,032.74	498.31	534.43	132,347.73
6	06/14/13	_____	1,032.74	496.30	536.44	131,811.29
7	07/14/13	_____	1,032.74	494.29	538.45	131,272.84
8	08/14/13	_____	1,032.74	492.27	540.47	130,732.37
9	09/14/13	_____	1,032.74	490.25	542.49	130,189.88
10	10/14/13	_____	1,032.74	488.21	544.53	129,645.35
11	11/14/13	_____	1,032.74	486.17	546.57	129,098.78
12	12/14/13	_____	1,032.74	484.12	548.62	128,550.16
Sub-total			12,392.88	5,943.04	6,449.84	128,550.16

New Home Buyer Amortization Schedule - Sample Home Mortgage
(Regular 15 Year): Monthly Payments for Last Year of Mortgage

169	01/14/27	1,032.74	45.36	987.38	11,108.91
170	02/14/27	1,032.74	41.66	991.08	10,117.83
171	03/14/27	1,032.74	37.94	994.80	9,123.03
172	04/14/27	1,032.74	34.21	998.53	8,124.50
173	05/14/27	1,032.74	30.47	1,002.27	7,122.23
174	06/14/27	1,032.74	26.71	1,006.03	6,116.20
175	07/14/27	1,032.74	22.94	1,009.80	5,106.40
176	08/14/27	1,032.74	19.15	1,013.59	4,092.81
177	09/14/27	1,032.74	15.35	1,017.39	3,075.42
178	10/14/27	1,032.74	11.53	1,021.21	2,054.21
179	11/14/27	1,032.74	7.70	1,025.04	1,029.17
180	12/14/27	1,032.74	3.86	1,029.17	0.00
Sub-total		12,393.17	296.88	12,096.29	0.00
Total		185,893.49	50,893.49	135,000.00	0.00

Facts regarding the reduced, 15-year mortgage technique of amortization to consider:

- It requires a fixed level of payment over the term which cannot be decreased without mortgage modification. However, should you have sufficient income and a desire to increase the payment for accelerated reduction of the mortgage at sometime in the future, this could most likely be accomplished without mortgage modification or prepayment penalty. However, check with your lender first before increasing payments.
- This method results in $4,857 greater interest savings than for the first technique described for payoff over a 15-year period. The trade off, though, is less flexibility. This technique requires a fixed payment over the term of the mortgage which is higher during the first seven and a half years than payments called for under the first technique described. Payments called for under the first technique start lower and gradually increase over the 15-year period.
- This technique is the most simple, requires the least attention, and results in the greatest interest savings.

As described in the examples for the three mortgage elimination techniques above, term reductions and interest savings can be significant, but nothing happens until you take initiative and start the process.

CHAPTER 7

The Money Value of Time Part One: Investing a Single Sum of Money over Time

The concept known as the time value of money is fundamental to the subject of finance. It is a broad subject, but I want to focus on its application to interest earned over time and compound interest (interest earned on interest). In this context, I believe that restating the concept can make it more easily understood. In my opinion, a more accurate and understandable phrasing of "the time value of money" in regards to interest earned over time and compound interest is "the money value of time." Such rephrasing more clearly reflects the fact that time affects the value of money. Young people and young adults have more time than anyone, and that is a strong advantage in the financial equation provided that time is harnessed positively.

I would like to explain the money value of time through the use of a simplified financial equation. Don't leave me now! I promise not to get into deep mathematical calculations (as if that were even possible for me to do) but will keep it simple and hopefully useful. Here it is, the financial equation, simplified, my version:

$$\text{Money x Rate of Return x Time} = \$\text{Outcome}$$

Granted, this is not an exact algebraic equation, and you can't plug numbers into it without some modification to solve for the $Outcome. However, this simple equation sets forth the key elements in computing a future sum or value. The point I want to make now is if you reduce the amount of time in the equation, you must increase the amount of money or rate of return to arrive at the same $Outcome.

The elements of this equation over which you will most likely have control are money and time. The one that you probably have the most control of right now, if you are a young adult, is time. And you may ask, what is so unusual about that? Everyone is young at some point in time, aren't they? Yes, that's true, but not everyone uses that youth (or time from youth to senior adulthood) to their advantage financially.

Now, let's use an example to demonstrate the effects that time and compound interest have on the $Outcome. Assume a single lump sum of $1,000 is invested at the beginning of four different time periods (10, 20, 30, and 40 years), and that the rate of return is 5% per year (high now but is below the average of 5.4% for 5-year FDIC insured certificates of deposit over the last 19 years). The outcomes for the four different time periods are as follows:

- $1,000 x 5% interest x 10 years = $1,629
- $1,000 x 5% interest x 20 years = $2,653
- $1,000 x 5% interest x 30 years = $4,321
- $1,000 x 5% interest x 40 years = $7,040

The $Outcome amounts may not seem significant to you yet, but when analyzed more closely the value of time becomes more clearly understood.

Let's relate our previous example to a person who is 25 years old. His objective is to accumulate $7,040 by age 65; however, he is evaluating whether he should start now at 25 and invest his $1,000 over 40 years or wait and invest over a 30-, 20-, or 10-year period when it may be easier to do so. At 25 years old $1,000 is not easy to come by, but he does have it. Expanding on the previous information from our example, his options are as follows:

Period	Investment Amount Required	Simple Interest Earnings	Compound Interest Earnings	Total Interest Earnings	$Outcome	Effective Annual Rate of Return on Initial Investment
40 year	$1,000	$2,000	$4,040	$6,040	$7,040	15.1%
30 year	$1,629	$2,444	$2,967	$5,411	$7,040	11.1%
20 year	$2,653	$2,653	$1,734	$4,387	$7,040	8.3%
10 year	$4,321	$2,161	$558	$2,719	$7,040	6.3%

From the above options, it appears clear the person should start now and choose the 40-year option. Why? Because at the 40-year period his investment is the lowest, and his rate of return is the highest. He puts in $1,000, time and interest earn $6,040, and his annual rate of return on his initial investment is 15.1% (not a bad return and remember we are talking about a 5%, 5-year bank CD). This return is computed by dividing the total return, $6,040, by 40 (40-year period) which equals $151, and dividing that amount by his initial investment of $1,000. For the purpose of the interest earnings, simple interest is computed by multiplying the investment amount by 5%, and that amount is multiplied by the number of years in the investment period. Compound interest, also known as the eighth wonder of the world, is interest earned on interest (a compounding factor for 5% was used to compute this amount).

What else can we learn from the above analysis? (Remember the objective of our example was to look at how time affects the $Outcome of money invested.) I can think of the following:

- The longer an amount is left to compound at interest, the higher the annual effective rate of return on the initial investment.
- The longer a person waits to invest, the more money they have to invest to achieve the same results as a smaller investment over a longer period of time. Hence,

time is making less for you and the investment costs you more. Expressed another way, the elements of the financial equation over which you have most control are time and money; if you reduce the amount of time, then you must increase the amount of money to achieve the same result.

- The earlier you start investing, the less risk you have to take to achieve acceptable, effective annual rates of return. For example, to earn an effective annual rate of 15% on your initial investment, it is highly unlikely that you could do that with insured bank CDs if you wait to invest over 10- or 20-year periods.

Take time to do some planning in your twenties or as early in life as you can. Ask your parents or grandparents to read this chapter of the book and give you their advice. Advice from the experienced can be very valuable but sometimes you have to ask for it.

The computations in this chapter were made using a compound interest table known as the "Single Sum of $1.00 Future Value Table." This table is presented at the end of this chapter. Use of this table is not complicated, and it is extremely beneficial for planning. For example, you can also use it for reverse computations, like what single sum do I need to invest now to have $20,000 in 10 years if the rate of interest I expect to earn is 5%? To obtain the answer, divide $20,000 by the table factor of 1.6289 (5% for 10 years) and the resulting amount is $12,278. I highly recommend you practice some calculations with this table and learn how easy it is to use. Remember, the compounding of interest is putting time to work making money for you.

In this chapter we have discussed the money value of time and the financial equation simplified. An example of investing a single sum of money over different periods of time was used to demonstrate the effects that time and compound interest have on the $Outcome of the investment. The bottom line is *start now, put time to work now, and reduce the need to invest more money later for the same results.*

Single-sum investing over different periods of time is one means to demonstrate the money value of time. In the next chapter, we will look at another means of investment, which is investing money regularly (monthly, weekly, etc.), to demonstrate the money value of time and of regular and consistent saving/ investing. This may be the point where you find you can jump in.

Future Value of $1

$FV = \$1\,(1 + i)^n$

n/i	1.0%	1.5%	2.0%	2.5%	3.0%	3.5%	4.0%	4.5%	5.0%	5.5%	6.0%	7.0%	8.0%	9.0%	10.0%
1	1.01000	1.01500	1.02000	1.02500	1.03000	1.03500	1.04000	1.04500	1.05000	1.05500	1.06000	1.07000	1.08000	1.09000	1.10000
2	1.02010	1.03022	1.04040	1.05063	1.06090	1.07123	1.08160	1.09203	1.10250	1.11303	1.12360	1.14490	1.16640	1.18810	1.21000
3	1.03030	1.04568	1.06121	1.07689	1.09273	1.10872	1.12486	1.14117	1.15763	1.17424	1.19102	1.22504	1.25971	1.29503	1.33100
4	1.04060	1.06136	1.08243	1.10381	1.12551	1.14752	1.16986	1.19252	1.21551	1.23882	1.26248	1.31080	1.36049	1.41158	1.46410
5	1.05101	1.07728	1.10408	1.13141	1.15927	1.18769	1.21665	1.24618	1.27628	1.30696	1.33823	1.40255	1.46933	1.53862	1.61051
6	1.06152	1.09344	1.12616	1.15969	1.19405	1.22926	1.26532	1.30226	1.34010	1.37884	1.41852	1.50073	1.58687	1.67710	1.77156
7	1.07214	1.10984	1.14869	1.18869	1.22987	1.27228	1.31593	1.36086	1.40710	1.45468	1.50363	1.60578	1.71382	1.82804	1.94872
8	1.08286	1.12649	1.17166	1.21840	1.26677	1.31681	1.36857	1.42210	1.47746	1.53469	1.59385	1.71819	1.85093	1.99256	2.14359
9	1.09369	1.14339	1.19509	1.24886	1.30477	1.36290	1.42331	1.48610	1.55133	1.61909	1.68948	1.83846	1.99900	2.17189	2.35795
10	1.10462	1.16054	1.21899	1.28008	1.34392	1.41060	1.48024	1.55297	1.62889	1.70814	1.79085	1.96715	2.15892	2.36736	2.59374
11	1.11567	1.17795	1.24337	1.31209	1.38423	1.45997	1.53945	1.62285	1.71034	1.80209	1.89830	2.10485	2.33164	2.58043	2.85312
12	1.12683	1.19562	1.26824	1.34489	1.42576	1.51107	1.60103	1.69588	1.79586	1.90121	2.01220	2.25219	2.51817	2.81266	3.13843
13	1.13809	1.21355	1.29361	1.37851	1.46853	1.56396	1.66507	1.77220	1.88565	2.00577	2.13293	2.40985	2.71962	3.06580	3.45227
14	1.14947	1.23176	1.31948	1.41297	1.51259	1.61869	1.73168	1.85194	1.97993	2.11609	2.26090	2.57853	2.93719	3.34173	3.79750
15	1.16097	1.25023	1.34587	1.44830	1.55797	1.67535	1.80094	1.93528	2.07893	2.23248	2.39656	2.75903	3.17217	3.64248	4.17725
16	1.17258	1.26899	1.37279	1.48451	1.60471	1.73399	1.87298	2.02237	2.18287	2.35526	2.54035	2.95216	3.42594	3.97031	4.59497

17	1.18430	1.28802	1.40024	1.52162	1.65285	1.79468	1.94790	2.1138	2.29202	2.48480	2.69277	3.15882	2.70002	4.32763	5.05447
18	1.19615	1.30734	1.42825	1.55966	1.70243	1.85749	2.02582	2.20848	2.40662	2.62147	2.85434	3.37993	3.99602	4.71712	5.55992
19	1.20811	1.32695	1.45681	1.59865	1.75351	1.92250	2.10685	2.30786	2.52695	2.76565	3.02560	3.61653	4.31570	5.14166	6.11591
20	1.22019	1.34686	1.48595	1.63862	1.80611	1.98979	2.19112	2.41171	2.65330	2.91776	3.20714	3.86968	4.66096	5.60441	6.72750
21	1.23239	1.36706	1.51567	1.67958	1.86029	2.05943	2.27877	2.52024	2.78596	3.07823	3.39956	4.14056	5.03383	6.10881	7.40025
25	1.28243	1.45095	1.64061	1.85394	2.09378	2.36324	2.66584	3.00543	3.38635	3.81339	4.29187	5.42743	6.84848	8.62308	10.83471
30	1.34785	1.56308	1.81136	2.09757	3.26204	2.80679	3.24340	3.74532	4.32194	4.98395	5.74349	7.61226	10.06266	13.26768	17.44940
40	1.48886	1.81402	2.20804	2.68506	3.26204	3.95926	4.80102	5.81636	7.03999	8.51331	10.28572	14.97446	21.72452	31.40942	45.25926

The Money Value of Time Part Two: Investing Sums of Money Regularly over Time

In this chapter we will look at investing money regularly (weekly, monthly) to demonstrate the money value of time and of regular and consistent saving/investing. In other words, this concept achieves the objective step by step and combines the power of the money value of time with saving/ investing regular amounts of money. This concept is also a common methodology for basic project management. Projects or objectives that appear overwhelming can often be accomplished more effectively by being broken down into smaller component pieces and addressed one at a time. Also, one of the advantages of this concept, or approach, is that it is a stress reliever. How, you might ask? It works like this: once a plan of action is put in place and a person begins to work it and see real progress, confidence that the objective can be reached results. And when confidence increases, stress decreases. It's as simple as that.

All right then, let's take on a financial project—an example of one, that is—and see how this works. Let's say you have done some planning (you remember this was suggested in the previous chapter). You expect to get married and have children and don't want to have empty pockets when your first child looks to you for help with a college education or to otherwise get a start in life when they are 18 years old. If you don't get married or have children you will have the money, so you win either way. Your financial project is to accumulate $50,000 in 18 years, your assumed rate of earnings is 3%, and you want to determine how much you would have to save/ invest on a monthly basis to accomplish your project. The simplified financial equation that I gave you in the previous chapter used to compute, or solve, for a future value was as follows:

$$\text{Money x Rate of Return x Time} = \$\text{Outcome}$$

In this example, we know the future value, or $Outcome, and estimated rate of return; therefore, we need to solve for the money required (monthly amount). In my opinion, the simplest means to perform the calculation and arrive at a result that is "close enough" for meaningful and effective planning is through use of the compound interest table known as "Future Value of an Ordinary Annuity of $1." A copy of this table is presented at the end of this chapter. That table is the tool we will use to solve our problem.

Now, let's get back to our problem. To compute the monthly amount required to be saved at 3% interest which will accumulate to $50,000 in 18 years, we first find the factor needed from the table under the column for 3.0% and the line (n/i) for 18, which is 23.4144. We then divide $50,000 by the factor of 23.4144 which equals the annual amount required of $2,135.43. The monthly requirement is obtained by dividing the annual requirement of $2,135.43 by 12 and is $177.95. The amount computed using a financial calculator that takes into consideration the compounding of interest month- by-month is $174.43. The difference from our table computation is only $3.52 per month, hence "close enough" for meaningful and effective planning, in my opinion. The results of our computations are as follows:

- Monthly payment required: $177.95.
- Total investment: $38,437.20 (216 monthly payments @ $177.95 per month).
- Total earnings: $11,562.80.
- Total accumulated sum: $50,000.00.

Over the 18-year period, you saved (month by month, $177.95 at a time) $38,437.10, which is a handsome sum of money and the result of consistent saving/investing over time. This result also demonstrates how a significant project can be accomplished by breaking it down into smaller, more manageable component pieces and dealing with one piece (in this case, a monthly investment) at a time. Also, let's not forget about the money value of time and wonder of compound interest which yielded $11,562.80 for you, or the accomplishment of 23% of the project task. Expressed another way, *you did three fourths of the work and time did one fourth*.

Compound interest is great, but to get its benefit you need to *start now* and put time to work to make money for you. I want to help make this process useful for you. You may be thinking that you would like to break this down into more manageable amounts now. Perhaps you are paid weekly and would rather make weekly saving/investment payments. Just divide the annual requirement in the previous example ($2,135.43) by 52, and the result is $41.07 per week.

I encourage you to spend some time planning using the future value table at the end of this chapter. That single table could be very valuable to you in the years to come.

Future Value of an Ordinary Annuity of $1

$$FVA = \frac{(1+i)^n - 1}{i}$$

n/i	1.0%	1.5%	2.0%	2.5%	3.0%	3.5%	4.0%	4.5%	5.0%	5.5%	6.0%	7.0%	8.0%	9.0%	10.0%
1	1.0000	1.0000	1.0000	1.0000	1.0000	1.0000	1.0000	1.0000	1.0000	1.0000	1.0000	1.0000	1.0000	1.0000	1.0000
2	2.0100	2.0150	2.0200	2.0250	2.0300	2.0350	2.0400	2.0450	2.0500	2.0550	2.0600	2.0700	2.0800	2.0900	2.1000
3	3.0301	3.0452	3.0604	3.0756	3.0909	3.1062	3.1216	3.1370	3.1525	3.1680	3.1836	3.2149	3.2464	3.2781	3.3100
4	4.0604	4.0909	4.1216	4.1525	4.1836	4.2149	4.2465	4.2782	4.3101	4.3423	4.3746	4.4399	4.5061	4.5731	4.6410
5	5.1010	5.1523	5.2040	5.2563	5.3091	5.3625	5.4163	5.4707	5.5256	5.5811	5.6371	5.7507	5.8666	5.9847	6.1051
6	6.1520	6.2296	6.3081	6.3877	6.4684	6.5502	6.6330	6.7169	6.8019	6.8881	6.9753	7.1533	7.3359	7.5233	7.7156
7	7.2135	7.3230	7.4343	7.5474	7.6625	7.7794	7.8983	8.0192	8.1420	8.2669	8.3938	8.6540	8.9228	9.2004	9.4872
8	8.2857	8.4328	8.5830	8.7361	8.8923	9.0517	9.2142	9.3800	9.5491	9.7216	9.8975	10.2598	10.6366	11.0285	11.4359
9	9.3685	9.5593	9.7546	9.9545	10.1591	10.3685	10.5828	10.8021	11.0266	11.2563	11.4913	11.9780	12.4876	13.0210	13.5795
10	10.4622	10.7027	10.9497	11.2034	11.4639	11.7314	12.0061	12.2882	12.5779	12.8754	13.1808	13.8164	14.4866	15.1929	15.9374
11	11.5668	11.8633	12.1687	12.4835	12.8078	13.1420	13.4864	13.8412	14.2068	14.5835	14.9716	15.7836	16.6455	17.5603	18.5312
12	12.6825	13.0412	13.4121	13.7956	14.1920	14.6020	15.0258	15.4640	15.9171	16.3856	16.8699	17.8885	18.9771	20.1407	21.3843
13	13.8093	14.2368	14.6803	15.1404	15.6178	16.1130	16.6268	17.1599	17.7130	18.2868	18.8821	20.1406	21.4953	22.9534	24.5227
14	14.9474	15.4505	15.9739	16.5190	17.0863	17.6770	18.2919	18.9321	19.5986	20.2926	21.0151	22.5505	24.2149	26.0192	27.9750
15	16.0969	16.6821	17.2934	17.9319	18.5989	19.2957	20.0236	20.7841	21.5786	22.4087	23.2760	25.1290	27.1521	29.3609	31.7725
16	17.2579	17.9324	18.6393	19.3802	20.1569	20.9710	21.8245	22.7193	23.6575	24.6411	25.6725	27.8881	30.3243	33.0034	35.9497

17	18.4304	19.2014	20.0121	20.8647	21.7616	22.7050	23.6975	24.7417	25.8404	26.9964	28.2129	30.8402	33.7502	36.9737	40.5447
18	19.6147	20.4894	21.4123	22.3863	23.4144	24.4997	25.6454	26.8551	28.1234	29.4812	30.9057	33.9990	37.4502	41.3013	45.5992
19	20.8109	21.7967	22.8406	23.9460	25.1169	26.3572	27.6712	29.0636	30.5390	32.1027	33.7600	37.3790	41.4463	46.0185	51.1591
20	22.0190	23.1237	24.2974	25.5447	26.8704	28.2797	29.7781	31.3714	33.0660	34.8683	36.7856	40.9955	45.7620	51.1601	57.2750
21	23.2392	24.4705	25.7833	27.1833	2836765	30.2695	31.9692	33.7831	35.7193	37.7861	39.9927	44.8652	50.4229	56.76485	64.0025
30	34.7849	37.5387	40.5681	43.9027	47.5754	51.6227	56.0849	61.0071	66.4388	72.4355	79.0582	94.4608	113.2832	136.3075	164.4940
40	48.8864	54.2679	60.4020	67.4026	75.4013	84.5503	95.0255	107.0303	120.7998	136.6056	154.7620	199.6351	259.0565	337.8824	442.5926

The Money Value of Time Part Three: Multiplying the $Outcome through Higher Rates of Return

I would like to start this chapter by restating my simplified financial equation:

$$\text{Money x Rate of Return x Time} = \$\text{Outcome}$$

As explained in chapter seven, this is not an exact algebraic equation but does set forth the key elements of computing a future sum or value. Also in chapter seven, the point was made that if the amount of time in the equation is reduced, the amount of money or rate of return must increase in order to have the same $Outcome. The elements of money and time and their effects on the $Outcome have been emphasized in chapters seven and eight. The element of rate of return and its effect on the $Outcome will be emphasized in this chapter.

Because the nature of the subject matter in this chapter may be considered more investment oriented than savings, I want to add a few words of clarification and caution. First, my objective in this chapter, consistent with chapters seven and eight, is to further explain compound interest calculations and the use of compound interest tables in financial planning with emphasis on higher rates of return. I am not a registered investment advisor and am not attempting to provide investment advice through this book. However, because higher rates of return are generally accompanied with higher rates of investment risk, I will provide a very limited introduction to investment risk in order to be realistic regarding the information presented. I am providing this information in order for readers to be aware that risk assessment is essential when reaching for higher returns. Further, I recommend a thorough risk assessment be performed in consultation with a competent and qualified investment advisor before implementing your long-term savings plan; please see chapter ten, "My Biggest Mistakes," for more suggestions regarding investment advisors.

As stated above, higher rates of return are generally accompanied with higher rates of risk. What kinds of risk, you may ask? Although not a complete list, the risks that an investment may not earn its expected return and/or may lose value of principal (the amount invested) are two very important ones. These risks are generally lowest when investing in regular FDIC insured accounts and certificates of deposit. Why, then, would you want to invest in anything else? Because the rates of return from the regular FDIC insured products may not be enough, together with the amount of money a person has to invest and the time period over which they have to invest it, to achieve their desired $Outcome.

Risks, therefore, have to be considered when reaching for higher returns. Why would someone take risks and expose themselves to the possibility of not earning the rate of return expected, or loss of principal? Normally it is because a person considers it is the most likely course of action to achieve their goal. A person may choose this course of action because they don't have enough time and money to plug into the financial equation to achieve the desired $Outcome at lower rates of return.

With all that said about risk, let's look at why higher returns motivate individuals to take higher risks. My conclusion on the matter is that when time is combined with higher returns, there are notably higher differences in the $Outcome. You may ask: Will you please give me a couple of examples of what you mean by notably higher differences? Sure, I am pleased that you asked. Let's see what differences result in investing at 5% and 10% over various periods. For our first example, let's invest a single sum of $1,000 over different time periods and see what notably higher differences result:

		Earnings Rate	Earnings Rate	Earnings Difference Between Rates	Higher Earnings
Amount invested	Time Period	5%	10%	Amount	Multiple
$1,000	10 years	$629	$1,594	$965	2.5
$1,000	20 years	$1,653	$5,727	$4,074	3.5
$1,000	30 years	$3,322	$16,449	$13,127	4.9
$1,000	40 years	$6,040	$44,259	$38,219	7.3

(Amounts for this example were computed using the "Future Value of $1" table presented at the end of chapter seven.)

Allow me to clarify the above information. First of all, yes, 10% is exactly double of 5%. However, per the above information, $1,000 invested for ten years at 10% earns 2.5 times the amount earned at 5%, and if invested at 10% for 20 years, it earns 3.5 times the amount invested at 5%, and 4.9 and 7.3 times for the 30 and 40 year investment periods. How do these multiples result? This is the money value of time and compound interest (interest earned on interest). Amazing!

For our second example, let's invest $1,200 a year at the end of each year over 10-, 20-, 30- and 40-year periods and compare our return differences at 5% and 10%:

		Earnings Rate	Earnings Rate	Earnings Difference Between Rates	Higher Earnings
Amount invested	Time Period	5%	10%	Amount	Multiple
$12,000	10 years	$3,094	$7,121	$4,027	2.3
$24,000	20 years	$15,679	$44,730	$29,051	2.9
$36,000	30 years	$43,726	$161,388	$117,662	3.7
$48,000	40 years	$96,960	$483,108	$386,148	5.0

(Amounts for this example were computed using the "Future Value of an Ordinary Annuity of $1" table presented at the end of chapter eight.)

Once again, time plus compound interest combine to produce higher return multiples at a 10% rate of return over 5% than the 2.0 multiples that might be expected. Also, the multiples in return differences continue to increase over time. And what about those dollar differences at 30 and 40 years? Incredible!

Let's summarize: *Because of the combined power of time and compound interest, investing at higher rates of return results in higher return multiples than simple rate comparisons alone reveal. These rate multiples also continue to increase over time.* Higher investment risks are also generally associated with higher rates of return and, therefore, should be taken into consideration when investing.

CHAPTER 10

My Biggest Mistakes: Learn at My Expense

Mistake #1: It was 1972. I was in my final quarter at Auburn University as an Accounting major and I learned while taking a "Time Value of Money" course that most adults have a 40-year working/saving period before they retire. I learned about and became fascinated with the concepts of compound interest. Yes, I learned about concepts like what a single sum could grow to if left to accumulate at interest over a 30-to 40-year period, or what the sum of an annuity (an amount invested regularly—yearly, monthly, etc.) could grow to in that length of time, or what notable differences resulted from investment returns of 10% vs. 5%. Sound familiar? (Hint: chapters seven through nine.)

So what did I do with that wonderful dynamic knowledge? My biggest mistake, here it is: I did little to nothing for ten years. I saved virtually nothing for ten years and accumulated debt. I must have sold the course book, as it is not in my library today. I threw away 10 years of the 40-year-working-and-saving period most adults have. At the time, I failed to recognize the importance and magnitude of what I am attempting to impress upon you now. The result is that I am having to save more money over the 30 years in my remaining work and saving period to have the same amount as someone who saved for 40 years. How much more? The answer is 80% more. Yes, that's right. And let me be clear: for someone who saved any sum of money in monthly sums over a 40-year period and earned 5% on their investment, I will have to invest 1.8 times that much monthly over 30 years to accumulate the same sum. The 10-year period from 30 to 40 years is sometimes referred to as the exponential period. If at all possible, don't miss it!

Mistake #2: As I explained in Mistake #1, I saved virtually nothing during my first ten years out of college. After that period, I did begin saving money. However, I did not establish a solid long-term plan for amounts saved. Specifically, I did not establish appropriate priorities for savings and set boundaries that would not be "trespassed." The most significant example I can remember is that I raided our children's college fund to increase the down payment on our second home (not that we had two homes, this was house two after house one) in order that our mortgage payments be lower. I reasoned that I had approximately nine years before the kids started college to pay it back and that would be enough time. It was but it required that saving for retirement be reduced during that period.

I believe a better solution would have been to spend less on house two and not "trespass" the boundary of the children's college fund. Having established boundaries is a safeguard of a well-prioritized, long-term saving plan and can help prevent important objectives from being thrown off course. A long-term savings plan should be somewhat flexible but, once put in place, any changes should be well thought out.

I highly recommend that you do not make the same mistake I did and instead establish a well-prioritized, long-term savings plan with appropriate boundaries (see chapter twelve for some examples of items to include). You may also want to get some additional help with this. One source for this type of assistance is Crown Financial Ministries whose website is Crown.org. Their product "The Money Map" costs $3.00 and is an excellent resource for establishing a long-term savings plan. "The Money Map" also incorporates several other financial objectives, such as establishing an emergency fund, paying off credit cards, pre-paying your mortgage, etc.

Mistake #3: I failed to consistently have on my side a competent and trustworthy investment advisor. I strongly encourage you to get as much investment education as you can but, unless you are in the investment business, you probably will not have enough time to devote to investment education that you would have no need of an advisor.

As I reached the point that I needed a greater rate of return on my investments than I could get on FDIC insured products, I turned to mutual funds. I did not try to pick them myself but instead used a recommended mutual fund investment newsletter service. The newsletter constructed portfolios based on a person's risk tolerance which was determined from a series of questions about a person's goals, age, appetite for risk, etc. The newsletter service tracked the performance of their portfolios and had a better-than-average track record. I generally found the service very helpful during *UP* markets. What I came to learn and experience, however, was that reading their advice about what to do in *DOWN* markets was not enough to keep me from making some serious mistakes. Emotions can take over sound reasoning when a person is losing money day after day for a prolonged period of time. That happened with me, two times that I can remember, in 2000 and 2009. A newsletter just did not provide the emotional support, together with sound guidance, that I needed to minimize costly mistakes. I have learned that a competent (generally well experienced) and trustworthy advisor can often provide the sound guidance that will aid in making better investment decisions during times of market and emotional turbulence.

I conclude that my long-term investments results would have been significantly better had I consistently engaged a competent and trustworthy investment advisor from the point I began to invest in the stock and bond markets. I humbly suggest that most of you reading this book would also fare better with their investments if they were to do the same.

Now I'll offer some practical comments and advice on selecting an advisor. First, it probably will not be easy. You may, in fact, go through a few before you settle on someone you believe best serves your needs. Generally, a fee-only advisor (charges a fee rather than a commission) or advisor paid a percentage of your account balance (usually not more than 1%) is more likely to recommend investments most suitable for you. Advisors, or brokers, compensated by commission only (they don't make any money unless you trade) are subject to conflicts of interest (conflicts between your interests and that of the advisor, the advisor's firm, etc.) by the nature of the compensation structure. Regardless of the compensation structure, you will only come to know the character and integrity of the advisor by working with them awhile.

Also, generally, the older and more experienced the advisor the better, for the obvious reasons. They have the battle experience and scars; they also tend to be more generous with their time. An advisor does not have to be on the verge of retirement but you should look for one with several years experience. Ask about their employment background. How long have they been in the investment business and who have they worked for? Always determine that they know what they are doing beforehand.

You may be thinking, when should I consider hiring an advisor? I think the opportune time is when you have constructed a long-term savings plan (see my Mistake #2 above). Having done that, you will have defined the objectives and will have simplified the job of the advisor. The advisor can then spend less time on trying to determine what you are trying to accomplish and more time on helping you select the proper investments to accomplish your objectives.

A final note on selecting an advisor: Ask your parents, grandparents, or other relatives or friends experienced in investment matters for a recommendation. I believe that I would have benefited from using my dad's advisor at least for a little while.

CHAPTER 11

Invest In Yourself

In this chapter I am writing to encourage you to consider investing in yourself educationally for financial reasons. In connection with selecting a career or a vocation, you have probably heard the exhortation "Do what you love, and the money will follow." I love to be outdoors, enjoying the hillsides, pastures, trees (autumn leaves especially), beaches, oceans, etc. I am sure you get the picture. I can get a little carried away with what I love or enjoy. But, the money has not been following me when I spent my time on those things. I was watching a documentary about the actor James Cagney a couple of years ago. As I remember, it was reported that he said something to the effect that acting enabled him to do what he loved. My thinking more closely parallels that reported statement. I would advise "Do what you are good at." It seems to follow that your income potential will be better when you do something well. For most, I think, doing what you are good at begins with doing what comes naturally or what you believe you are gifted or best suited for. The next step, in my opinion, is to develop and perfect your abilities, which requires education/training and experience.

Let's pause for just a second and focus. I am not a career counselor but am sharing my insights and what I have learned from research which concludes that, generally speaking, higher income follows higher educational levels. The subject area of this book is personal finance, and my comments in this chapter relate to improving your personal finances, namely income, through investing in education for yourself. So, if you are interested in investing in education for the purpose of increasing your income, I believe information in this chapter may be helpful to you. Please know, however, if you have or are planning to invest in education for reasons other than increasing your income, I am not writing to discourage you from doing that. Again, my purpose for addressing this subject is to make you aware that, on the whole, higher income follows higher education levels.

The United States Census Bureau has compiled, from what I have been able to find, the most comprehensive and understandable statistics on education and its financial value. Their most recent publishing of this information entitled "What It's Worth: Field of Training and Economic Status in 2009" was issued in February of 2012[1]. You can obtain the report easily by doing an Internet search for the title. I am not going to attempt to address all subject matter covered in their publication but rather certain points I consider significant. These were the following:

- All postsecondary educational levels of the U.S. population are increasing significantly. The publication states "In 2009, 45 percent of the adult population (aged 18 and older) had a degree or certificate above the high school level, up from 21 percent in 1984. This increase resulted from an increase in the proportion of the population with postsecondary educational attainment at all levels, from vocational certificates to doctorate degrees." (Ewert 2)
- The highest increase in postsecondary credentials from 1984 to 2009 was for vocational certificates which increased from 1.8 percent to 10.9 percent of the adult population. That is huge and represents a six fold increase.

[1] Ewert, Stephanie. "What It's Worth: Field of Training and Economic Status in 2009." *Household Economic Studies.* February, 2012: 1-16. http://www.census.gov/prod/2012pubs/p70-129.pdf

- Most of the postsecondary credentials held and mean or average monthly earnings for each level of credential were as follows:

	Number	Mean Monthly Earnings
Vocational certificate	24,709,000	$3,538
Associate's Degree	18,429,000	$4,166
Bachelor's Degree	38,782,000	$5,445
Master's Degree	15,132,000	$6,731

(As indicated for the above levels of credential, mean monthly earnings increase as the level of credential increases.)

- Completing high school also pays off. The mean monthly earnings for high school graduates was $3,179, which was $745 more than for those who attended but did not complete high school.

A summary of the points presented above is as follows:

1) There is a trend among the U.S. adult population to earn higher educational credentials.
2) The higher the credential, the higher the pay.
3) Even completing high school pays off.

It seems to reason that if the overall work force is becoming more educated, then for a person to effectively compete in that environment he/she must invest in education. It's also my opinion (not a subject of the Census Bureau publication) that continuing education in one's field of study after completing their desired level of educational credential is also a means of increasing one's economic value. Expressed another way, for most, a person's job or vocation is their primary economic engine. Therefore, it makes sense to keep it tuned up.

I hope the above information has been helpful relative to the economic value of investing in yourself via education. I encourage you to read the Census Bureau publication in its entirety. There is information about various fields of study in addition to the general information I shared with you. I also encourage you to seriously consider whether investing in education makes sense for you and to evaluate available options.

CHAPTER 12

Set Your Course and Write It Down

Most young adults have time to reach their goals. Is it necessary that they put them in writing? According to a recent study conducted by Dr. Gail Matthews at Dominican University of California, the answer appears clearly to be *yes*. Her study, which can be found online, in my view, was basically a study of those with unwritten goals, those with written goals, and those with written goals and accountability. The results which appeared most significant to me were the following:

- Those with written goals accomplished approximately 50% more than those with unwritten goals.
- Those with written goals, action commitments, and written accountability to a supportive friend accomplished approximately 25% more than those with written goals and approximately 78% more than those with unwritten goals.

I am motivated by 50% results just by putting goals in writing, and I hope you will be also.

Why does this process of writing down goals work, or why is it so impacting? I can think of the following reasons:

- I believe as human beings we are wired that way. From the *King James Bible*[2], we find an exhortation to the prophet Habakkuk. It reads, "Write the vision and make it plain upon tables, that he may run that readeth it" (Hab. 2.2). Notice the verse includes the word "run." Could

[2] *The Holy Bible, King James Version.* New York: Oxford Edition: 1769; *King James Bible Online*, 2008. http://www.kingjamesbibleonline.org/

that imply that a written vision inspires a higher level of achievement? I think that is a reasonable interpretation.

- I believe that when a person commits to achieving a goal, he has engaged accountability. Accountability, whether to a superior (boss, supportive friend, etc.) or to a goal, prompts a person to strive for results, knowing that achievement of results brings a reward and failure to do so brings undesirable consequences.

- Accountability to goals can be engaged and is extremely practical and productive on a daily basis. My term for working with goals on a daily basis is "list management." Make a list of things to do, prioritize the items, and check them off as you get them done. Such a process gives you a sense of accomplishment and a means for achieving higher results.

- I believe that the process of developing and using goals and related action steps educates a person as to the importance of achieving the smaller intermediate steps which eventually result in achieving the overall goal. For example, suppose a salesman has set a goal of $75,000 a year in commission earnings and that he earns 10% commission on his product sales. He therefore needs to sell $750,000 in product over the year to meet his goal or $62,500 in product sales per month. By breaking down his sales goal into monthly amounts, he makes the process more manageable. As he achieves his monthly goals, those he can more realistically get his arms around, he will eventually (by year end) achieve his annual goal. This salesman could even go further with this process in order to bring it down to the smallest steps that need to be accomplished. If he knows on average that it takes twenty sales calls to sell $10,000 in product, he then knows he must make on average 125 calls per month or approximately thirty two calls per week in order to sell approximately $62,500 in product per month.

- I believe that what you keep in front of you, focus on, and practice affects your decision making. As you regularly read over and focus on your goals while implementing action steps to accomplish them, I believe your decision making is affected. Relative to personal finance, goals and related action steps help discipline and guide you, shape your financial thinking, and reduce the occurrence of bad financial decisions. Further, well-defined goals help you prioritize your financial life and set your boundaries. By having such safe guards certain troublesome issues are avoided because you "don't even go there". For example, if you have determined to live on a cash basis, you do not shop for a car with the intention of immediately buying it unless you have the cash to pay for it. In this case, affordability of monthly payments no longer guides you but rather contentment of true ownership. Certain clients and friends of mine have had "buyer's remorse" over purchasing new cars on credit. Save yourself the grief; you may find as I have that riding in "peace" is better than riding in "style."

I encourage you to put the odds in your favor by writing your goals down and keeping them in front of you. My current pastor has his written on poster board which he has placed on the wall near his bedroom. My wife has hers on what she calls her "Dreamboard". I have mine in a notebook with pictures related to the goals. The point is to keep them in a place where you will look at them often.

Let me give you a few ideas for goals and related action steps. The goals are the numbered items and the action steps are described aside the bullets:

1. Live within your means on a cash basis.

    *   Create an annual budget (chapter two).
    *   From an annual budget, create a monthly budget before each month begins.
    *   Monitor actual expenses each week and each month using the Monthly Resource Management Worksheet (chapter three).

2. Eliminate consumer debts.

    *   Implement a strategic payment plan to eliminate consumer debts (chapter five).

3. Establish an emergency fund of at least three months living expenses.

    *   Establish a savings account.
    *   Have a garage sale and/or Internet sale for household items to get the fund started.
    *   Save a pre-established amount of money every pay period.
    *   Set up an automatic transfer from checking to savings/ MMA for amounts saved each pay period.

4. Payoff home mortgage debt in half the remaining term.

    *   Implement a mortgage elimination technique that adds next month's principal to the current month's payment (chapter six).

5. Establish a long-term savings plan to include savings goals for retirement and children's college tuition and begin funding.

- Compute total amounts needed, how much to save per month to fund, and appropriate investments. You may need professional help for this.
- If your employer has a retirement plan such as a 401(K) plan and will match what you save up to a certain percentage of salary, it generally makes sense to do that. A match of this nature is, in effect, a 100% return on what you have saved.
- Monitor status of goal accomplishment each year and revise goals and funding if necessary.

6. Establish a fund for helping others.

- Determine the types of needs you would like to provide assistance for.
- Set a dollar amount per year or percentage of your income as your goal.
- Include the amount or estimated amount in your annual and monthly budget.
- Set up a monthly automatic transfer from your checking account to an account established for this purpose.

7. Consider furthering your career or vocational education (see chapter eleven)

- Do an Internet search for the United States Census Bureau publication entitled "What It's Worth: Field of Training and Economic Status in 2009." Read the publication and find out what people are earning in various fields of study.
- Finish high school if you have not already done so.
- Search for and evaluate options to further your education.

Some may choose to work on items four and five at the same time. That's an individual call. Paying off your mortgage, however, is a guaranteed return (you save those interest dollars when you pay principal early), and most often at a higher rate than you can get on a safe savings investment such as a FDIC insured certificate of deposit. If you are concerned about using up cash, consider securing a line of credit on your home for the equity created by paying down the mortgage (assuming the equity is significant). Should cash flow become tight, the line of credit could be tapped for funds needed. Payoff the line of credit as soon as possible.

Should you adopt the above goals, you may choose to work on all or some of them to begin with. The order presented for goals one, two, and three is a logical priority order in which to accomplish them in my opinion. If your cash flow permits, and your employer offers a retirement plan match (under goal five), I would do that as soon as possible assuming the plan investments are solid. Check with your employer's plan administrator and your own investment advisor about this.

I would recommend computing amounts required for goals four and five next. The order in which you work on them is an individual call. One of the results of managing your money wisely may well be a surplus. If this is the case, you may find that goal number six is one that is compelling and fulfilling to you.

. . .

I would like to close this chapter and book with what I consider realistic advice on developing goals and action steps to engage one or many of the concepts and methodologies covered thus far. My recommendations are:

- Reject confusion, fear, procrastination, or any other emotion that causes you to freeze up and not act. Muster the determination to move forward.

- Take a few minutes (literally) and note the items from the text you believe would help *you* the most—just the subject matter, not goals or action steps.
- If you don't have much time to devote to the process now, start with one item from your list. For that one item, write down your goal and action step(s) and implement whatever steps you document. Also, make a note on your calendar at some future date when you will revisit the overall list you made. At that time, consider taking on another item from your list and engaging the goal/action steps process.
- If you have time and are motivated to get going with many of the concepts and methodologies in this book, I suggest you begin with a getaway session. Perhaps take a long weekend some place quiet. Take the subject matter list I recommended above and from it start drafting your goals and action steps. But be sure to take breaks during the process. Go out for a walk, have a cup of coffee, etc. The idea is to remain fresh. When you recognize your focus and effectiveness waning during the drafting process, stop what you are doing and divorce yourself from the process. Then pick up again later in the day or the next day when you are rested.

Once you have finished drafting your goals and action steps, plan time to implement them. I suggest you schedule time and write it on your calendar. Enjoy the rest of your getaway and then go home and get to work on implementation. If one getaway session is not enough, plan another. Or if you can, spend a quiet day at home. Stay with the process until you address all the subject matter that is important to you. But just remember that whether you start with one goal and related action steps or many, I urge you to *start now*!

www.ingramcontent.com/pod-product-compliance
Lightning Source LLC
Chambersburg PA
CBHW022128170526
45157CB00004B/1800